HENRY

HENRY VAUGHAN

Selected Poems

edited with an introduction by
Robert B. Shaw

Fyfield Books

FOR EVELYN
AND IN MEMORY OF JAY

First published in 1976, reprinted in 1983
New format edition in 1992 by
Carcanet Press Limited
208–212 Corn Exchange Buildings
Manchester M4 3BQ

A CIP catalogue record for this book is available
from the British Library.
ISBN 0 85635 139 3

The Publisher acknowledges financial assistance
from the Arts Council of Great Britain.

Printed and bound in England by SRP Ltd, Exeter

CONTENTS

Introduction

Henry Vaughan's reputation probably stands higher today than at any time since his death. During a long life which spanned the years from 1621 to 1695 he enjoyed only a brief celebrity, and that confined to the coterie of Mrs Katherine Phillips, the 'matchless Orinda'. Geography, politics and the movements of taste abetted one another in promoting Vaughan's obscurity. Except for two years at Oxford (1638-40) and the two following in London, during which time he studied law and gained what acquaintance he had of literary society, Vaughan resided in his native Wales, far removed from a literary milieu. (It is possible that his natural tongue was Welsh, a circumstance which would have distanced him more than geographically from the centre of English letters.) The Civil War, which prompted Vaughan's return from London, also created unusually turbulent conditions for the emergence of a new poetic talent. A determined Royalist, Vaughan may have seen some service in the conflict in the years preceding the appearance of his first volumes of verse. *Poems, with the tenth Satyre of Iuvenal Englished* (1646) and *Olor Iscanus* (apparently complete in 1647, but only published in 1651) did not go beyond a first edition. *Silex Scintillans*, published in 1650, did not do so either; but the unsold sheets were bound for reissue in 1655 with some additional poems which formed Part II of a volume identically titled. It is on this book of religious verse that Vaughan's claim to literary distinction now rests. But these poems of mystical devotion stirred little interest in the Restoration period. The concerns of poetry were becoming increasingly secular, and Vaughan's metaphysical wit must have appeared cumbrously oldfashioned compared to the pointed couplets of the new satire. Vaughan seems to have written less after issuing the enlarged *Silex Scintillans*. He had established

7

himself as a practitioner not of law but of medicine; when he began and what training he had we do not know. In 1673 he wrote to John Aubrey that he had 'practised for many years with good success'. *Thalia Rediviva*, a return to the secular subjects of his first two books, appeared in 1678. Besides his poems he published during the 1650's several prose works, most of them translations of devotional and medical treatises. *The Mount of Olives: or, Solitary Devotions* (1652), although it draws upon other writers, is the most original piece of Vaughan's prose. It is valuable as a confirming witness to the religious temper which *Silex Scintillans* suggests – that of a solitary, a stranger in the world.

The Puritan proscription of Anglican services certainly was a proximate cause of Vaughan's resort to 'Solitary Devotions'. But his own inclinations tended to the same end; the pattern of isolation which we observe in his outward biography is present in his inner life as well. He strives to imitate Christ who, he says in *The Mount of Olives*, 'in the day-time taught and preach'd, but continued all night in prayer, sometimes in a Mountain apart, sometimes amongst the wild beasts, and sometimes in solitary places'. In poem after poem he seeks, as a night watcher, the mystical colloquy in which one deep calls unto another. This sense of standing singly and simply before God very likely derives from Vaughan's conviction that God had singled him out with a particular providence. The major event of his life was the Pauline conversion he underwent at some time in the years before *Silex Scintillans* appeared: an event, in fact, which may have turned him to the writing of religious poetry. In a title page engraving to *Silex Scintillans* and in a Latin poem which accompanies it, Vaughan depicts the experience. The emblem is of the Arm of God issuing from a cloud, wielding the steel which strikes fire from a heart-shaped flint — the 'silex scintillans' of the title. Flame bursts up from the heart of stone while drops of liquid (blood? tears? — apparently both) pour down from it. In the

Latin poem the iconography is explained: all of God's gentler persuasions having failed to allure Vaughan's obdurate heart, he now attacks with terrible force, turning stone to suffering flesh. As a result,

> *Coelosq; tuos ardentia tandem*
> Fragmenta, & *liquidas ex* Adamante *genas.*

'The fragments flame toward Thy Heaven and Thee, and my cheeks stream with tears wrung from the adamant.' The poems which follow are certainly informed both with ardours of praise and tears of contrition. Vaughan ends his Latin verses by declaring himself, 'in the wreckage of my worldly fortunes,' all the richer for the divine chastisement.

Some recent scholars have expressed doubts about the authenticity of Vaughan's conversion as he describes it, suggesting that he overdramatizes his spiritual experience to provide an arresting rationale for religious lyrics he would have written in any case. Although there is no way to decide such a question for certain, it seems wisest to me to take Vaughan at his word. Such a sudden invasion of grace would not be out of keeping with his contemplative nature; he was a man who felt things deeply, and entirely in his own way. Notably, he is the only one of the great religious poets of his time to witness publicly to a Pauline conversion. The arguments against the reality or centrality of this event are generally tied to attempts to invest Vaughan's secular verse with a greater stature than most of his readers are willing to allow. There will always be critics who rejoice not to concur with the common reader. I am not one of them. All of the poems but two in my selection are taken from *Silex Scintillans.*

Taking Vaughan at his word, of course, is not to say that he experienced the power of God in a vacuum, totally unaffected by external events. He glances at these himself

9

in speaking of the 'wreckage' in the midst of which he newly experiences God's grace. He may refer to a serious illness from which he suffered around this time, or perhaps generally to the devastations of the Civil War. The death of his younger brother William in 1648 is an even stronger possibility. William Vaughan may well have died of wounds sustained in the conflict. The series of untitled elegies scattered through *Silex Scintillans* is apparently for him. All of these data have significance. Grace does not disdain the aid of nature in perfecting its designs. What chiefly matters is that Vaughan found himself inwardly transformed and in consequence wrote poems which he would not otherwise have written.

*

It is much easier to sense the unique flavour of Vaughan's finest poems than it is to define it. Critics have made us perhaps overly aware of the sources and influences present in Vaughan's lines. I would argue that these presences, pervasive though they may be, are not dominating. The most noticeable influence on Vaughan's style — one that is hard not to notice — is that of Herbert. Vaughan was not at pains to conceal his indebtedness. The preface to the 1655 edition of *Silex Scintillans* speaks of 'that blessed man, Mr. George Herbert, whose holy *life* and *verse* gained many pious Converts, (of whom I am the least) . . .' Herbert made quite as considerable a contribution to the verbal surface of Vaughan's poems as to his spiritual development. F. E. Hutchinson has said that there is no other instance in English literature of one poet's borrowing, with only slight alteration, the very phrases of another. Most readers would agree that when Vaughan closely models an entire poem upon one of Herbert's he is not at his best. The real danger of influence is not, of course, in verbal echoes. It is rather that the earlier poet's treatment of a subject may have such authority as to block his disciple from achieving any compelling vision of it. 'Unprofitablenes', a poem not

10

included in this selection, is a case in which Vaughan rather
mechanically adapts one of Herbert's greatest poems, 'The
Flower'. Herbert begins,

> How fresh, O Lord, how sweet and clean
> Are thy returns! ev'n as the flowers in spring;
> To which, besides their own demean,
> The late-past frosts tributes of pleasure bring.
> > Grief melts away
> > Like snow in May,
> As if there were no such cold thing.

Similarly Vaughan:

> How rich, O Lord! how fresh thy visits are!
> 'Twas but Just now my black leaves hopeless hung
> > Sullyed with dust and mud . . .

Herbert subtly develops his image in a poem of fifty lines,
following the flower through times of sun and frost, the
influx of grace and its withholding. His dominant mood is
one of hope ('And now in age I bud again, / After so many
deaths I live and write . . .') and he ends with a moral which
his experience has verified:

> These are thy wonders, Lord of love,
> To make us see we are but flowers that glide:
> Which when we once can finde and prove,
> Thou hast a garden for us, where to bide.
> > Who would be more,
> > Swelling through store,
> Forfeit their Paradise by their pride.

To Herbert's fifty lines Vaughan has a crowded eighteen,
and he develops the image with a morbid self-absorption
which deprives it of the depth it has in Herbert. He ends
with a note of personal melancholy rather than a
generalized application:

11

But, ah, my God! what fruit hast thou of this?
What one poor leaf did ever I yet fall
        To wait upon thy wreath?
Thus thou all day a thankless weed doest dress,
And when th'hast done, a stench, or fog is all
        The odour I bequeath.

It would be easy enough to find other examples of Vaughan's perfunctorily borrowing Herbert's themes and imagery, and then failing to exploit their full potential. But it should be apparent to any reader that Herbert's influence operated more often to the good of Vaughan's work than to its detriment. It is clearly Herbert who provided the precedent for a style at once intimate and highly formal; the achievement of the poems lies in their maintaining a conversational tone while at the same time meeting the demands of stanzaic intricacy. Vaughan can employ colloquial effects as brilliantly as Herbert, often beginning his poems with a striking abruptness: 'I saw Eternity the other night.' He has, moreover, his own particular preoccupations, and in dealing with these his own voice, quite distinct from Herbert's, is fully in command.

Among influences other than Herbert's, critics have pointed with special attention to the Hermetic philosophy, a body of occult speculation which by the mid-seventeenth century had deeply marked both science and metaphysics. Hermeticism probably would not have recognized the distinction made in a phrase like 'both science and metaphysics'. It viewed all things as comprising a unity in God, and conceived the spirit of God as present in all his creatures, animate or inanimate. During the years when Vaughan wrote most of his poetry his twin brother Thomas, under the pen-name Eugenius Philalethes, was one of the most energetic promoters of Hermetic thought in England. Thomas Vaughan made his own alchemical experiments and disseminated his own theories together with those of the full range of Hermetic writers, from the mythical Hermes

Trismegistus down to Paracelsus and Cornelius Agrippa. The titles of some of his books suggest the extent of his concerns and the arcane approach he took to them: *Anthroposophia Theomagica* ('Or a Discourse on the Nature of Man and his state after Death; Grounded on his Creator's Proto-Chemistry and verifi'd by a practicall Examination of Principles in the Great World'); *Anima Magica Abscondita* ('Or a Discourse of the universall Spirit of Nature'); *Magica Adamica* ('Or the Antiquitie of Magic'). If Henry Vaughan had become as absorbed in esoteric studies as his beloved brother did, his verse might have no more than an antiquarian interest. Fortunately he has employed Hermetic themes and vocabulary with selectivity and tact, and it is in only a few poems that knowledge of these is essential to our understanding. The premiss of 'Cock-crowing', for instance, is that a sympathetic bond exists between each earthly object and a celestial counterpart; in a rooster this property is a 'Sunnie seed' whose 'magnetisme' causes the bird to await and respond to the first rays of the sun. Vaughan's emphasis on light, here and elsewhere, is in keeping with Hermetic practice, but it is of course an imagery readily available within the mainstream of the Christian tradition. Similarly, although Hermetic notions of an indwelling spirit in all creatures lead Vaughan to speak of inanimate objects such as stones and trees as sentient, he buttresses his vision with biblical references. In a poem like 'And do they so?' he is indulging himself not in a flight of fancy but in absolute textual literalness, drawing out the implications of St Paul's statement that 'the whole creation' looks for the coming of Christ 'in groaning and travail'.

Vaughan's reading of the bible, in fact, must surely have made the deepest impression on his verse of any of his supposed sources. The bible is his 'one *Pearle* by whose light / All things I see' ('Silence, and stealth of days!'). The scriptural passages cited at the head or, more frequently, at the end of a given poem are neither idly chosen nor gratuitously reproduced. In its several English and Latin versions the bible furnishes Vaughan not only with numerous turns of phrase but with a vital centre round which style, thought and imagery gravitate and from which they derive much of their energy. It is this deep grounding in scripture which allows the poems, however private their devotional impulse, to be participated in by the reader rather than merely overheard.

Once due weight has been given to Vaughan's indebtedness to the writings of others, it remains to account for the discipline by which he assembles disparate fragments of tradition to form such highly individualized utterances. Vaughan has accomplished this feat, it seems to me, because his imaginative powers were focused upon a single presiding theme, almost to the exclusion of any other. This theme, in keeping with the retiring nature of his character, is the theme of alienation. I use this term in an older and more radical sense than the one employed by Marxist theoreticians. Vaughan is at odds not merely with society but with the entire physical cosmos in which it is his lot to live. The model of the Christian which he adopts from the New Testament is that of a stranger and a pilgrim in this world, finding here 'no continuing city', journeying toward 'an house not made with hands, eternal in the heavens'. His impatience with the visible creation is his chief point of difference from Herbert. Hazarding a generalization, we may say that Herbert is a sacramentalist, perceiving grace as dispensed through the agency of created things, while Vaughan is a mystic of the Negative Way, to whom all conditions of mortality are barriers between his soul and God. Both of these approaches, of course, have ancient sanction in the Church, and one is rarely pursued to the total exclusion of the other. Which course is the more emphasized is probably determined in each individual as much by temperament as by conviction. Herbert, in his poem called 'Man', celebrates the glories of creation: 'Oh mightie love! Man is one world, and hath / Another to attend him.' He concludes with a petition delicately balanced between man's present duty and future expectation.

> Since then, my God, thou hast
> So brave a Palace built; O dwell in it,
> That it may dwell with thee at last!
> Till then, afford us so much wit;
> That, as the world serves us, we may serve thee,
> And both thy servants be.

But Vaughan, in his poem of the same name, cannot see in nature even a temporary home for so restless a creature as man:

> Man is the shuttle, to whose winding quest
> And passage through these looms
> God order'd motion, but ordain'd no rest.

The consuming longing to be free of the incommodities of the flesh colours Vaughan's treatment of two subjects in which critics have long noticed his special interest: nature and childhood. In his dealing with these themes Vaughan has been thought a precursor of Wordsworth, but differences in the two poets' outlooks weigh heavier than similarities. Although he had an affectionate eye for landscape (as we may see in the charming lines 'To my worthy friend Master T. Lewes'), nature could never be the comfort to Vaughan that it was to Wordsworth. The Hermetic notion of a divine spark dwelling in all things is always qualified in Vaughan's religious poems by the idea that natural appearances are a veil marking our estrangement from God. The obedience within the divine order of those creatures inferior to man stands as a constant reproach to man's waywardness. Notes of celebration are sobered by those of penitence. In the case of childhood, too, the reflection upon past glories yields to an anxious hope of renewed innocence in the future. Vaughan is not so much concerned to idealize a particular time of his life as he is to lament his exile from the Paradise

15

which both the bible and Boethius (whose own lament Vaughan translated) have taught men to mourn. The focus again is turned on things to come, on the Kingdom of Heaven which, in Christ's words, a man may enter only if he 'become as a little child'. This is Vaughan's hoped-for destination, 'That shady City of Palme trees', as he calls it in 'The Retreate'. It can finally be attained only beyond this life, but in the 'death' of the mystical moment a man may have a foretaste of its joys. Such a moment is what Vaughan pleads for at the end of 'Regeneration': 'Lord, then said I, *On me one breath, / And let me dye before my death!'*

It is in poems like 'They are all gone into the world of light!' and in the elegies for his brother William that Vaughan's turning from this world is most poignantly voiced: 'And I alone sit lingring here.' Such poems remind us that his prized solitude was never sought as an end in itself but as a path to communion with God and with his Saints. It is likely that these poems will carry a special resonance for Christians who are accustomed to pray for the faithful departed, giving thanks for the spirits of just men made perfect. But I should think that readers of any persuasion would be moved by them. It is a universal impulse, and not merely a Christian one, which inspires men to raise up something lasting out of loss.

From *Olor Iscanus* (1651)

To my worthy friend Master *T. Lewes*

Sees not my friend, what a deep snow
Candies our Countries wooddy brow?
The yeelding branch his load scarse bears
Opprest with snow, and *frozen tears*,
While the *dumb* rivers slowly float,
All bound up in an *Icie Coat.*
  Let us meet then! and while this world
In wild *Excentricks* now is hurld,
Keep wee, like nature, the same *Key*,
And walk in our forefathers way;
Why any more cast wee an Eye
On what *may come*, not what is *nigh?*
Why vex our selves with *feare*, or *hope*
And cares beyond our *Horoscope?*
Who into future times would peere
Looks oft beyond his terme set here,
And cannot goe into those grounds
But through a *Church-yard* which them bounds;
Sorrows and sighes and searches spend
And draw our bottome to an end,
But discreet Joyes lengthen the lease
Without which life were a disease,
And who this age a Mourner goes,
Doth with his tears but feed his foes.

Metrum 5

Happy that first white age! when wee
Lived by the Earths meere Charitie,
No soft luxurious Diet then
Had Effeminated men,
No other meat, nor wine had any
Then the Course Mast, or simple honey,
And by the Parents care layd up
Cheap *Berries* did the Children sup.

19

No pompous weare was in those dayes
Of gummie Silks, or Skarlet bayes,
Their beds were on some flowrie brink
And clear Spring-water was their drink.
The shadie Pine in the Suns heat
Was their Coole and known Retreat,
For then 'twas not cut down, but stood
The youth and glory of the wood.
The daring Sailer with his slaves
Then had not cut the swelling waves,
Nor for desire of forraign store
Seen any but his native shore.
No stirring Drum had scarr'd that age,
Nor the shrill Trumpets active rage,
No wounds by bitter hatred made
With warm bloud soil'd the shining blade;
For how could hostile madness arm
An age of love to publick harm?
When Common Justice none withstood,
Nor sought rewards for spilling bloud.
  O that at length our age would raise
Into the temper of those dayes!
But (worse then *AEtna's* fires!) debate
And Avarice inflame our state.
Alas! who was it that first found
Gold hid of purpose under ground,
That sought out Pearles, and div'd to find
Such pretious perils for mankind!

From *Silex Scintillans*, Part I (1650)

Regeneration

A Ward, and still in bonds, one day
                    I stole abroad,
It was high-spring, and all the way
          Primros'd, and hung with shade;
          Yet, was it frost within,
                    And surly winds
Blasted my infant buds, and sinne
          Like Clouds ecclips'd my mind.

2

Storm'd thus; I straight perceiv'd my spring
                    Meere stage, and show,
My walke a monstrous, mountain'd thing
          Rough-cast with Rocks, and snow;
          And as a Pilgrims Eye
                    Far from reliefe,
Measures the melancholy skye
          Then drops, and rains for griefe,

3

So sigh'd I upwards still, at last
                    'Twixt steps, and falls
I reach'd the pinacle, where plac'd
          I found a paire of scales,
          I tooke them up and layd
                    In th'one late paines,
The other smoake, and pleasures weigh'd
          But prov'd the heavier graines;

4

With that, some cryed, *Away*; straight I
                    Obey'd, and led
Full East, a faire, fresh field could spy
          Some call'd it, *Jacobs Bed*;
          A Virgin-soile, which no

Rude feet ere trod,
Where (since he stept there,) only go
Prophets, and friends of God.

5

Here, I repos'd; but scarse well set,
A grove descryed
Of stately height, whose branches met
And mixt on every side;
I entred, and once in
(Amaz'd to see't,)
Found all was chang'd, and a new spring
Did all my senses greet;

6

The unthrift Sunne shot vitall gold
A thousand peeces,
And heaven its azure did unfold
Checqur'd with snowie fleeces,
The aire was all in spice
And every bush
A garland wore; Thus fed my Eyes
But all the Eare lay hush.

7

Only a little Fountain lent
Some use for Eares,
And on the dumbe shades language spent
The Musick of her teares;
I drew her neere, and found
The Cisterne full
Of divers stones, some bright, and round
Others ill-shap'd, and dull.

8

The first (pray marke,) as quick as light
Danc'd through the floud,
But, th'last more heavy then the night

Nail'd to the Center stood;
I wonder'd much, but tyr'd
At last with thought,
My restless Eye that still desir'd
As strange an object brought;

9

It was a banke of flowers, where I descried
(Though 'twas mid-day,)
Some fast asleepe, others broad-eyed
And taking in the Ray,
Here musing long, I heard
A rushing wind
Which still increas'd, but whence it stirr'd
No where I could not find;

10

I turn'd me round, and to each shade
Dispatch'd an Eye,
To see, if any leafe had made
Least motion, or Reply,
But while I listning sought
My mind to ease
By knowing, where 'twas, or where not,
It whisper'd; *Where I please.*

Lord, then said I, *On me one breath,
And let me dye before my death!*

Cant. Cap. 5. ver. 17
Arise O North, and come thou South-wind, and blow upon my garden, that the spices thereof may flow out.

The Showre

'Twas so, I saw thy birth: That drowsie Lake
From her faint bosome breath'd thee, the disease
Of her sick waters, and Infectious Ease.
      But, now at Even
      Too grosse for heaven,
Thou fall'st in teares, and weep'st for thy mistake.

2

Ah! it is so with me; oft have I prest
Heaven with a lazie breath, but fruitles this
Peirc'd not; Love only can with quick accesse
      Unlock the way,
      When all else stray
The smoke, and Exhalations of the brest.

3

Yet, if as thou doest melt, and with thy traine
Of drops make soft the Earth, my eyes could weep
O're my hard heart, that's bound up, and asleep,
      Perhaps at last
      (Some such showres past,)
My God would give a Sun-shine after raine.

Vanity of Spirit

Quite spent with thoughts I left my Cell, and lay
Where a shrill spring tun'd to the early day.
    I beg'd here long, and gron'd to know
    Who gave the Clouds so brave a bow,
    Who bent the spheres, and circled in
    Corruption with this glorious Ring,
    What is his name, and how I might
    Descry some part of his great light.
I summon'd nature: peirc'd through all her store,
Broke up some seales, which none had touch'd before,

Her wombe, her bosome, and her head
Where all her secrets lay a bed
I rifled quite, and having past
Through all the Creatures, came at last
To search my selfe, where I did find
Traces, and sounds of a strange kind.
Here of this mighty spring, I found some drills,
With Ecchoes beaten from th' eternall hills;
Weake beames, and fires flash'd to my sight,
Like a young East, or Moone-shine night,
Which shew'd me in a nook cast by
A peece of much antiquity,
With Hyerogliphicks quite dismembred,
And broken letters scarce remembred.
I tooke them up, and (much Joy'd,) went about
T' unite those peeces, hoping to find out
The mystery; but this neer done,
That little light I had was gone:
It griev'd me much. At last, said I,
Since in these veyls my Ecclips'd Eye
May not approach thee, (for at night
Who can have commerce with the light?)
I'le disapparell, and to buy
But one half glaunce, most gladly dye.

The Retreate

Happy those early dayes! when I
Shin'd in my Angell-infancy.
Before I understood this place
Appointed for my second race,
Or taught my soul to fancy ought
But a white, Celestiall thought,
When yet I had not walkt above
A mile, or two, from my first love,
And looking back (at that short space,)
Could see a glimpse of his bright-face;

26

When on some *gilded Cloud*, or *flowre*
My gazing soul would dwell an houre,
And in those weaker glories spy
Some shadows of eternity;
Before I taught my tongue to wound
My Conscience with a sinfull sound,
Or had the black art to dispence
A sev'rall sinne to ev'ry sence,
But felt through all this fleshly dresse
Bright *shootes* of everlastingnesse.
  O how I long to travell back
And tread again that ancient track!
That I might once more reach that plaine,
Where first I left my glorious traine,
From whence th' Inlightned spirit sees
That shady City of Palme trees;
But (ah!) my soul with too much stay
Is drunk, and staggers in the way.
Some men a forward motion love,
But I by backward steps would move,
And when this dust falls to the urn
In that state I came return.

¶

Come, come, what doe I here?
    Since he is gone
Each day is grown a dozen year,
    And each houre, one;
    Come, come!
  Cut off the sum,
  By these soil'd teares!
  (Which only thou
  Know'st to be true,)
  Dayes are my feares.

2

Ther's not a wind can stir,
    Or beam passe by,
But strait I think (though far,)
    Thy hand is nigh;
      Come, come!
    Strike these lips dumb:
    This restles breath
    That soiles thy name,
    Will ne'r be tame
    Untill in death.

3

Perhaps some think a tombe
    No house of store,
But a dark, and seal'd up wombe,
    Which ne'r breeds more.
      Come, come!
    Such thoughts benum;
    But I would be
    With him I weep
    A bed, and sleep
    To wake in thee.

¶ Midnight

When to my Eyes
(Whilst deep sleep others catches,)
    Thine hoast of spyes
The starres shine in their watches,
    I doe survey
    Each busie Ray,
And how they work, and wind,
    And wish each beame
    My soul doth streame,
With the like ardour shin'd;
    What Emanations,

Quick vibrations
And bright stirs are there?
What thin Ejections,
Cold Affections,
And slow motions here?

2
Thy heav'ns (some say,)
Are a firie-liquid light,
Which mingling aye
Streams, and flames thus to the sight.
Come then, my god!
Shine on this bloud,
And water in one beame,
And thou shalt see
Kindled by thee
Both liquors burne, and streame.
O what bright quicknes,
Active brightnes,
And celestiall flowes
Will follow after
On that water,
Which thy spirit blowes!

Math. Cap. 3. ver. xi
I indeed baptize you with water unto repentance, but he that commeth after me, is mightier than I, whose shooes I am not worthy to beare, he shall baptize you with the holy Ghost, and with fire.

¶ Content

Peace, peace! I know 'twas brave,
But this corse fleece
I shelter in, is slave
To no such peece.
When I am gone,

I shall no ward-robes leave
        To friend, or sonne
But what their own homes weave,

2

Such, though not proud, nor full,
        May make them weep,
And mourn to see the wooll
        Outlast the sheep;
        Poore, Pious weare!
Hadst thou bin rich, or fine
        Perhaps that teare
Had mourn'd thy losse, not mine.

3

Why then these curl'd, puff'd points,
        Or a laced story?
Death sets all out of Joint
        And scornes their glory;
        Some Love a *Rose*
In hand, some in the skin;
        But crosse to those,
I would have mine *within*.

¶

Joy of my life! while left me here,
        And still my Love!
How in thy absence thou dost steere
        Me from above!
        A life well lead
        This truth commends,
        With quick, or dead
        It never ends.

2

Stars are of mighty use: The night

Is dark, and long;
The Rode foul, and where one goes right,
Six may go wrong.
One twinkling ray
Shot o'r some cloud,
May clear much way
And guide a croud.

3

Gods Saints are shining lights: who stays
Here long must passe
O're dark hills, swift streames, and steep ways
As smooth as glasse;
But these all night
Like Candles, shed
Their beams, and light
Us into Bed.

4

They are (indeed,) our Pillar-fires
Seen as we go,
They are that Cities shining spires
We travell too;
A swordlike gleame
Kept man for sin
First *Out*; This beame
Will guide him *In*.

The Storm

I see the use: and know my bloud
Is not a Sea,
But a shallow, bounded floud
Though red as he;
Yet have I flows, as strong as his,
And boyling stremes that rave
With the same curling force, and hisse,

As doth the mountain'd wave.

2

But when his waters billow thus,
        Dark storms, and wind
Incite them to that fierce discusse,
        Else not Inclin'd,
Thus the Enlarg'd, inraged air
        Uncalmes these to a floud,
But still the weather that's most fair
        Breeds tempests in my bloud;

3

Lord, then round me with weeping Clouds,
        And let my mind
In quick blasts sigh beneath those shrouds
        A spirit-wind,
So shall that storme purge this *Recluse*
        Which sinfull ease made foul,
And *wind*, and *water* to thy use
        Both *wash*, and *wing* my soul.

The Morning-watch

O Joyes! Infinite sweetnes! with what flowres,
And shoots of glory, my soul breakes, and buds!
        All the long houres
        Of night, and Rest
        Through the still shrouds
        Of sleep, and Clouds,
    This Dew fell on my Breast;
        O how it *Blouds*,
And *Spirits* all my Earth! heark! In what Rings,
And *Hymning Circulations* the quick world
        Awakes, and sings;
        The rising winds,
        And falling springs,

Birds, beasts, all things
Adore him in their kinds.
Thus all is hurl'd
In sacred *Hymnes*, and *Order*, The great *Chime*
And *Symphony* of nature. Prayer is
The world in tune,
A spirit-voyce,
And vocall joyes
Whose *Eccho is* heav'ns blisse.
O let me climbe
When I lye down! The Pious soul by night
Is like a clouded starre, whose beames though sed
To shed their light
Under some Cloud
Yet are above,
And shine, and move
Beyond that mistie shrowd.
So in my Bed
That Curtain'd grave, though sleep, like ashes, hide
My lamp, and life, both shall in thee abide.

The Evening-watch

A Dialogue

Farewell! I goe to sleep; but when   *Body*
The day-star springs, I'le wake agen.

Goe, sleep in peace; and when thou lyest   *Soul*
Unnumber'd in thy dust, when all this frame
Is but one dramme, and what thou now descriest
In sev'rall parts shall want a name,
Then may his peace be with thee, and each dust
Writ in his book, who ne'r betray'd mans trust!

Amen! but hark, e'r we two stray,   *Body*
How many hours do'st think 'till day?

33

Ah! go; th'art weak, and sleepie. Heav'n *So*
Is a plain watch, and without figures winds
All ages up; who drew this Circle even
     He fils it; Dayes, and hours are *Blinds*.
Yet, this take with thee; The last gasp of time
Is thy first breath, and mans *eternall Prime*.

¶

Silence, and stealth of dayes! 'tis now
     Since thou art gone,
Twelve hundred houres, and not a brow
     But Clouds hang on
As he that in some Caves thick damp
     Lockt from the light,
Fixeth a solitary lamp,
     To brave the night
And walking from his Sun, when past
     That glim'ring Ray
Cuts through the heavy mists in haste
     Back to his day,
So o'r fled minutes I retreat
     Unto that hour
Which shew'd thee last, but did defeat
     Thy light, and pow'r,
I search, and rack my soul to see
     Those beams again,
But nothing but the snuff to me
     Appeareth plain;
That dark, and dead sleeps in its known,
     And common urn,
But those fled to their Makers throne,
     There shine, and burn;
O could I track them! but souls must
     Track one the other,
And now the spirit, not the dust
     Must be thy brother.

34

Yet I have one *Pearle* by whose light
      All things I see,
And in the heart of Earth, and night
      Find Heaven, and thee.

Peace

My Soul, there is a Countrie
      Far beyond the stars,
Where stands a winged Centrie
      All skilfull in the wars,
There above noise, and danger
      Sweet peace sits crown'd with smiles,
And one born in a Manger
      Commands the Beauteous files,
He is thy gracious friend,
      And (O my Soul awake!)
Did in pure love descend
      To die here for thy sake,
If thou canst get but thither,
      There growes the flowre of peace,
The Rose that cannot wither,
      Thy fortresse, and thy ease;
Leave then thy foolish ranges;
      For none can thee secure,
But one, who never changes,
      Thy God, thy life, thy Cure.

The Passion

O my chief good!
My dear, dear God!
When thy blest bloud
Did Issue forth forc'd by the Rod,
What pain didst thou
Feel in each blow!
How didst thou weep,

35

And thy self steep
In thy own precious, saving teares!
What cruell smart
Did teare thy heart!
How didst thou grone it
In the spirit,
O thou, whom my soul Loves, and feares!

2

Most blessed Vine!
Whose juice so good
I feel as Wine,
But thy faire branches felt as bloud,
How wert thou prest
To be my feast!
In what deep anguish
Didst thou languish,
What springs of Sweat, and bloud did drown thee!
How in one path
Did the full wrath
Of thy great Father
Crowd, and gather,
Doubling thy griefs, when none would own thee!

3

How did the weight
Of all our sinnes,
And death unite
To wrench, and Rack thy blessed limbes!
How pale, and bloudie
Lookt thy Body!
How bruis'd, and broke
With every stroke!
How meek, and patient was thy spirit!
How didst thou cry,
And grone on high
Father forgive,
And let them live,

I dye to make my foes inherit!

4

O blessed Lamb!
That took'st my sinne,
That took'st my shame
How shall thy dust thy praises sing!
I would I were
One hearty tear!
One constant spring!
Then would I bring
Thee two small mites, and be at strife
Which should most vie,
My heart, or eye,
Teaching my years
In smiles, and tears
To weep, to sing, thy *Death*, my *Life*.

Rom. Cap. 8. ver. 19

*Etenim res Creatae exerto Capite observantes expectant
revelationem Filiorum Dei.*

And do they so? have they a Sense
Of ought but Influence?
Can they their heads lift, and expect,
And grone too? why th'Elect
Can do no more: my volumes sed
They were all dull, and dead,
They judg'd·them senslesse, and their state
Wholly Inanimate.
Go, go; Seal up thy looks,
And burn thy books.

2

I would I were a stone, or tree,
    Or flowre by pedigree,
Or some poor high-way herb, or Spring
    To flow, or bird to sing!
Then should I (tyed to one sure state,)
    All day expect my date;
But I am sadly loose, and stray
    A giddy blast each way;
      O let me not thus range!
         Thou canst not change.

3

Sometimes I sit with thee, and tarry
    An hour, or so, then vary.
Thy other Creatures in this Scene
    Thee only aym, and mean;
Some rise to seek thee, and with heads
    Erect peep from their beds;
Others, whose birth is in the tomb,
    And cannot quit the womb,
      Sigh there, and grone for thee,
        Their liberty.

4

O let not me do lesse! shall they
    Watch, while I sleep, or play?
Shall I thy mercies still abuse
    With fancies, friends, or newes?
O brook it not! thy bloud is mine,
    And my soul should be thine;
O brook it not! why wilt thou stop
    After whole showres one drop?
      Sure, thou wilt joy to see
        Thy sheep with thee.

Corruption

Sure, It was so. Man in those early days
    Was not all stone, and Earth,
He shin'd a little, and by those weak Rays
    Had some glimpse of his birth.
He saw Heaven o'r his head, and knew from whenc
    He came (condemned,) hither,
And, as first Love draws strongest, so from hence
    His mind sure progress'd thither.
Things here were strange unto him: Swet, and till
    All was a thorn, or weed,
Nor did those last, but (like himself,) dyed still
    As soon as they did *Seed*,
They seem'd to quarrel with him; for that Act
    That fel him, foyl'd them all,
He drew the Curse upon the world, and Crackt
    The whole frame with his fall.
This made him long for *home*, as loath to stay
    With murmurers, and foes;
He sigh'd for *Eden*, and would often say

    Ah! what bright days were those?
Nor was Heav'n cold unto him; for each day
    The vally, or the Mountain
Afforded visits, and still *Paradise* lay
    In some green shade, or fountain.
Angels lay *Leiger* here; Each Bush, and Cel,
    Each Oke, and high-way knew them,
Walk but the fields, or sit down at some *wel*,
    And he was sure to view them.
Almighty *Love*! where art thou now? mad man
    Sits down, and freezeth on,
He raves, and swears to stir nor fire, nor fan,
    But bids the thread be spun.
I see, thy Curtains are Close-drawn; Thy bow
    Looks dim too in the Cloud,
Sin triumphs still, and man is sunk below
    The Center, and his shrowd;

All's in deep sleep, and night; Thick darknes lyes
          And hatcheth o'r thy people;
But hark! what trumpets that? what Angel cries
          Arise! Thrust in thy sickle.

Son-dayes

Bright shadows of true Rest! some shoots of blisse,
                    Heaven once a week;
The next worlds gladnes prepossest in this;
                    A day to seek

Eternity in time; the steps by which
We Climb above all ages; Lamps that light
Man through his heap of dark days; and the rich,
And full redemption of the whole weeks flight.

2

The Pulleys unto headlong man; times bower;
                    The narrow way;
Transplanted Paradise; Gods walking houre;
                    The Cool o'th' day;

The Creatures *Jubile*; Gods parle with dust;
Heaven here; Man on those hills of Myrrh, and flowres;
Angels descending; the Returns of Trust;
A gleam of glory, after six-days-showres.

3

The Churches love-feasts; Times Prerogative,
                    And Interest
Deducted from the whole; The Combs, and hive,
                    And home of rest.

The milky way Chalkt out with Suns; a Clue
That guides through erring hours; and in full story
A taste of Heav'n on earth; the pledge, and Cue

Of a full feast; And the Out Courts of glory.

The BURIAL Of an Infant

Blest Infant Bud, whose Blossome-life
Did only look about, and fal,
Wearyed out in a harmles strife
Of tears, and milk, the food of all;

Sweetly didst thou expire: Thy soul
Flew home unstain'd by his new kin,
For ere thou knew'st how to be foul,
Death *wean'd* thee from the world, and sin.

Softly rest all thy Virgin-Crums!
Lapt in the sweets of thy young breath,
Expecting till thy Saviour Comes
To *dresse* them, and *unswadle* death.

Faith

Bright, and blest beame! whose strong projection
    Equall to all,
Reacheth as well things of dejection
    As th' high, and tall;
How hath my God by raying thee
    Inlarg'd his spouse,
And of a private familie
    Made open house?
All may be now Co-heirs; no noise
    Of *Bond*, or *Free*
Can Interdict us from those Joys
    That wait on thee,
The Law, and Ceremonies made
    A glorious night,
Where Stars, and Clouds, both light, and shade

Had equal right;
But, as in nature, when the day
        Breaks, night adjourns,
Stars shut up shop, mists pack away,
        And the Moon mourns;
So when the Sun of righteousness
        Did once appear,
That Scene was chang'd, and a new dresse
        Left for us here;
Veiles became useles, Altars fel,
        Fires smoking die;
And all that sacred pomp, and shel
        Of things did flie;
Then did he shine forth, whose sad fall,
        And bitter fights
Were figur'd in those mystical,
        And Cloudie Rites;
And as i'th' natural Sun, these three,
        Light, motion, heat,
So are now *Faith, Hope, Charity*
        Through him Compleat;
Faith spans up blisse; what sin, and death
        Put us quite from,
Lest we should run for't out of breath,
        Faith brings us home;
So that I need no more, but say
        I do believe,
And my most loving Lord straitway
        Doth answer, *Live.*

The Tempest

How is man parcell'd out? how ev'ry hour
        Shews him himself, or somthing he should see?
        This late, long heat may his Instruction be,
And tempests have more in them than a showr.

        When nature on her bosome saw

42

Her Infants die,
And all her flowres wither'd to straw,
Her brests grown dry;
She made the Earth their nurse, & tomb,
Sigh to the sky,
'Til to those sighes fetch'd from her womb
Rain did reply,
So in the midst of all her fears
And faint requests
Her Earnest sighes procur'd her tears
And fill'd her brests.

O that man could do so! that he would hear
The world read to him! all the vast expence
In the Creation shed, and slav'd to sence
Makes up but lectures for his eie, and ear.

Sure, mighty love foreseeing the discent
Of this poor Creature, by a gracious art
Hid in these low things snares to gain his heart,
And layd surprizes in each Element.

All things here shew him heaven; *Waters* that fall
Chide, and fly up; *Mists* of corruptest fome
Quit their first beds & mount; trees, herbs, flowres, all
Strive upwards stil, and point him the way home.

How do they cast off grossness? only *Earth*,
And *Man* (like *Issachar*) in lodes delight,
Water's refin'd to *Motion*, Aire to *Light*,
Fire to all *three, but man hath no such mirth.

Plants in the *root* with Earth do most Comply,
Their *Leafs* with water, and humiditie,
The *Flowres* to air draw neer, and subtiltie,
And *seeds* a kinred fire have with the sky.

All have their *keyes*, and set *ascents*; but man

43

Though he knows these, and hath more of his own,
    Sleeps at the ladders foot; alas! what can
These new discoveries do, except they drown?

Thus groveling in the shade, and darkness, he
    Sinks to a dead oblivion; and though all
    He sees, (like *Pyramids,*) shoot from this ball
And less'ning still grow up invisibly,

Yet hugs he stil his durt; The *stuffe* he wears
    And painted trimming takes down both his eies,
    Heaven hath less beauty than the dust he spies,
And money better musick than the *Spheres.*

Life's but a blast, he knows it; what? shal straw,
    And bul-rush-fetters temper his short hour?
    Must he nor sip, nor sing? grows ne'r a flowr
To crown his temples? shal dreams be his law?

O foolish man! how hast thou lost thy sight?
    How is it that the Sun to thee alone
    Is grown thick darkness, and thy bread, a stone?
Hath flesh no softness now? mid-day no light?

Lord! thou didst put a soul here; If I must
    Be broke again, for flints will give no fire
    Without a steel, O let thy power cleer
Thy gift once more, and grind this flint to dust!
*Light, Motion, Heat.

The Pilgrimage

As travellours when the twilight's come,
And in the sky the stars appear,
The past daies accidents do summe
With, *Thus wee saw there, and thus here.*

Then *Jacob*-like lodge in a place

44

(A place, and no more, is set down,)
Where till the day restore the race
They rest and dream homes of their own.

So for this night I linger here,
And full of tossings too and fro,
Expect stil when thou wilt appear
That I may get me up, and go.

I long, and grone, and grieve for thee,
For thee my words, my tears do gush,
O that I were but where I see!
Is all the note within my Bush.

As Birds rob'd of their native wood,
Although their Diet may be fine,
Yet neither sing, nor like their food,
But with the thought of home do pine;

So do I mourn, and hang my head,
And though thou dost me fullnes give,
Yet look I for far better bread
Because by this man cannot live.

O feed me then! and since I may
Have yet more days, more nights to Count,
So strengthen me, Lord, all the way,
That I may travel to thy Mount.

Heb. Cap.xi. ver.13

*And they confessed, that they were strangers and Pilgrims
on the earth.*

The World

I saw Eternity the other night
Like a great *Ring* of pure and endless light,

All calm, as it was bright,
And round beneath it, Time in hours, days, years
            Driv'n by the spheres
Like a vast shadow mov'd, In which the world
            And all her train were hurl'd;
The doting Lover in his queintest strain
            Did their Complain,
Neer him, his Lute, his fancy, and his flights,
            Wits sour delights,
With gloves, and knots the silly snares of pleasure
            Yet his dear Treasure
All scatter'd lay, while he his eys did pour
            Upon a flowr.

2

The darksome States-man hung with weights and woe
Like a thick midnight-fog mov'd there so slow
            He did nor stay, nor go;
Condemning thoughts (like sad Ecclipses) scowl
            Upon his soul,
And Clouds of crying witnesses without
            Pursued him with one shout.
Yet dig'd the Mole, and lest his ways be found
            Workt under ground,
Where he did Clutch his prey, but one did see
            That policie,
Churches and altars fed him, Perjuries
            Were gnats and flies,
It rain'd about him bloud and tears, but he
            Drank them as free.

3

The fearfull miser on a heap of rust
Sate pining all his life there, did scarce trust
            His own hands with the dust,
Yet would not place one peece above, but lives
            In feare of theeves.
Thousands there were as frantick as himself

And hug'd each one his pelf,
The down-right Epicure plac'd heav'n in sense
        And scornd pretence
While others slipt into a wide Excesse
        Said little lesse;
The weaker sort slight, triviall wares Inslave
        Who think them brave,
And poor, despised truth sate Counting by
        Their victory.

4

Yet some, who all this while did weep and sing,
And sing, and weep, soar'd up into the *Ring*,
    But most would use no wing.
O fools (said I,) thus to prefer dark night
        Before true light,
To live in grots, and caves, and hate the day
        Because it shews the way,
The way which from this dead and dark abode
        Leads up to God,
A way where you might tread the Sun, and be
        More bright than he.
But as I did their madnes so discusse
        One whisper'd thus,
This Ring the Bride-groome did for none provide
        But for his bride.

John Cap. 2. ver. 16, 17

All that is in the world, the lust of the flesh, the lust of the Eys, and the pride of life, is not of the father, but is of the world.

And the world passeth away, and the lusts thereof, but he that doth the will of God abideth for ever.

47

The Constellation

Fair, order'd lights (whose motion without noise
    Resembles those true Joys
Whose spring is on that hil where you do grow
    And we here tast sometimes below,)

With what exact obedience do you move
    Now beneath, and now above,
And in your vast progressions overlook
    The darkest night, and closest nook!

Some nights I see you in the gladsome East,
    Some others neer the West,
And when I cannot see, yet do you shine
    And beat about your endles line.

Silence, and light, and watchfulnes with you
    Attend and wind the Clue,
No sleep, nor sloth assailes you, but poor man
    Still either sleeps, or slips his span.

He grops beneath here, and with restless Care
    First makes, then hugs a snare,
Adores dead dust, sets heart on Corne and grass
    But seldom doth make heav'n his glass.

Musick and mirth (if there be musick here)
    Take up, and tune his year,
These things are Kin to him, and must be had,
    Who kneels, or sighs a life is mad.

Perhaps some nights hee'l watch with you, and peep
    When it were best to sleep,
Dares know Effects, and Judge them long before,
    When th' herb he treads knows much, much more.

But seeks he your *Obedience, Order, Light,*

Your calm and wel-train'd flight,
Where, though the glory differ in each star,
    Yet is there peace still, and no war?

Since plac'd by him who calls you by your names
    And fixt there all your flames,
Without Command you never acted ought
    And then you in your Courses fought.

But here Commission'd by a black self-wil
    The sons the father kil,
The Children Chase the mother, and would heal
    The wounds they give, by crying, zeale.

Then Cast her bloud, and tears upon thy book
    Where they for fashion look,
And like that Lamb which had the Dragons voice
    Seem mild, but are known by their noise.

Thus by our lusts disorder'd into wars
    Our guides prove wandring stars,
Which for these mists, and black days were reserv'd,
    What time we from our first love swerv'd.

Yet O for his sake who sits now by thee
    All crown'd with victory,
So guide us through this Darknes, that we may
    Be more and more in love with day;

Settle, and fix our hearts, that we may move
    In order, peace, and love,
And taught obedience by thy whole Creation,
    Become an humble, holy nation.

Give to thy spouse her perfect, and pure dress,
    Beauty and *holiness*,
And so repair these Rents, that men may see
And say, *Where God is, all agree.*

The Shepheards

Sweet, harmles livers! (on whose holy leisure
    Waits Innocence and pleasure,)
Whose leaders to those pastures, and cleer springs,
    Were *Patriarchs*, Saints, and Kings,
How happend it that in the dead of night
    You only saw true light,
While *Palestine* was fast a sleep, and lay
    Without one thought of Day?
Was it because those first and blessed swains
    Were pilgrims on those plains
When they receiv'd the promise, for which now
    'Twas there first shown to you?
'Tis true, he loves that Dust whereon they go
    That serve him here below,
And therefore might for memory of those
    His love there first disclose;
But wretched *Salem* once his love, must now
    No voice, nor vision know,
Her stately Piles with all their height and pride
    Now languished and died,
And *Bethlems* humble Cotts above them stept
    While all her Seers slept;
Her Cedar, firr, hew'd stones and gold were all
    Polluted through their fall,
And those once sacred mansions were now
    Meer emptiness and show,
This made the Angel call at reeds and thatch,
    Yet where the shepheards watch,
And Gods own lodging (though he could not lack,)
    To be a common *Rack*;
No costly pride, no soft-cloath'd luxurie
    In those thin Cels could lie,
Each stirring wind and storm blew through their Cots
    Which never harbour'd plots,
Only Content, and love, and humble joys
    Lived there without all noise,

Perhaps some harmless Cares for the next day
    Did in their bosomes play,
As where to lead their sheep, what silent nook,
    What springs or shades to look,
But that was all; And now with gladsome care
    They for the town prepare,
They leave their flock, and in a busie talk
    All towards *Bethlem* walk
To see their souls great shepheard, who was come
    To bring all straglers home,
Where now they find him out, and taught before
    That Lamb of God adore,
That Lamb whose daies great Kings and Prophets wish'd
    And long'd to see, but miss'd.
The first light they beheld was bright and gay
    And turn'd their night to day,
But to this later light they saw in him,
    Their day was dark, and dim.

Mount of Olives

When first I saw true beauty, and thy Joys
Active as light, and calm without all noise
Shin'd on my soul, I felt through all my powr's
Such a rich air of sweets, as Evening showrs
Fand by a gentle gale Convey and breath
On some parch'd bank, crown'd with a flowrie wreath;
Odors, and Myrrh, and balm in one rich floud
O'r-ran my heart, and spirited my bloud,
My thoughts did swim in Comforts, and mine eie
Confest, *The world did only paint and lie.*
And where before I did no safe Course steer
But wander'd under tempests all the year,
Went bleak and bare in body as in mind,
And was blow'n through by ev'ry storm and wind,
I am so warm'd now by this glance on me,
That, midst all storms I feel a Ray of thee;

51

So have I known some beauteous *Paisage* rise
In suddain flowres and arbours to my Eies,
And in the depth and dead of winter bring
To my Cold thoughts a lively sense of spring.

   Thus fed by thee, who dost all beings nourish,
My wither'd leafs again look green and flourish,
I shine and shelter underneath thy wing
Where sick with love I strive thy name to sing,
Thy glorious name! which grant I may so do
That these may be thy *Praise*, and my *Joy* too.

Man

Weighing the stedfastness and state
Of some mean things which here below reside,
Where birds like watchful Clocks the noiseless date
    And Intercourse of times divide,
Where Bees at night get home and hive, and flowrs
    Early, aswel as late,
Rise with the Sun, and set in the same bowrs;

2

I would (said I) my God would give
The staidness of these things to man! for these
To his divine appointments ever cleave,
    And no new business breaks their peace;
The birds nor sow, nor reap, yet sup and dine,
    The flowres without clothes live,
Yet *Solomon* was never drest so fine.

3

Man hath stil either toyes, or Care,
He hath no root, nor to one place is ty'd,
But ever restless and Irregular
    About this Earth doth run and ride,
He knows he hath a home, but scarce knows where,
    He sayes it is so far

52

That he hath quite forgot how to go there.

4

He knocks at all doors, strays and roams,
Nay hath not so much wit as some stones have
Which in the darkest nights point to their homes,
By some hid sense their Maker gave;
Man is the shuttle, to whose winding quest
And passage through these looms
God order'd motion, but ordain'd no rest.

¶

I walkt the other day (to spend my hour)
Into a field
Where I sometimes had seen the soil to yield
A gallant flowre,
But Winter now had ruffled all the bowre
And curious store
I knew there heretofore.

2

Yet I whose search lov'd not to peep and peer
I'th' face of things
Thought with my self, there might be other springs
Besides this here
Which, like cold friends, sees us but once a year,
And so the flowre
Might have some other bowre.

3

Then taking up what I could neerest spie
I digg'd about

That place where I had seen him to grow out,
And by and by

I saw the warm Recluse alone to lie
      Where fresh and green
    He lived of us unseen.

4

Many a question Intricate and rare
      Did I there strow,
But all I could extort was, that he now
      Did there repair
Such losses as befel him in this air
      And would e'r long
    Come forth most fair and young.

5

This past, I threw the Clothes quite o'r his head,
      And stung with fear
Of my own frailty dropt down many a tear
      Upon his bed,
Then sighing whisper'd, *Happy are the dead!*
      What peace doth now
    Rock him asleep below?

6

And yet, how few believe such doctrine springs
      From a poor root
Which all the Winter sleeps here under foot
      And hath no wings
To raise it to the truth and light of things,
      But is stil trod
    By ev'ry wandring clod.

7

O thou! whose spirit did at first inflame
      And warm the dead,
And by a sacred Incubation fed
      With life this frame
Which once had neither being, forme, nor name,
      Grant I may so

Thy steps track here below,

8

That in these Masques and shadows I may see
      Thy sacred way,
And by those hid ascents climb to that day
      Which breaks from thee
Who art in all things, though invisibly;
      Shew me thy peace,
    Thy mercy, love, and ease,

9

And from this Care, where dreams and sorrows raign
      Lead me above
Where Light, Joy, Leisure, and true Comforts move
      Without all pain,
There, hid in thee, shew me his life again
      At whose dumbe urn
    Thus all the year I mourn.

From *Silex Scintillans*, Part II (1655)

Ascension-Hymn

Dust and clay
Mans antient wear!
Here you must stay,
But I elsewhere;
Souls sojourn here, but may not rest;
Who will ascend, must be undrest.

And yet some
That know to die
Before death come,
Walk to the skie
Even in this life; but all such can
Leave behinde them the old Man.

If a star
Should leave the Sphaere,
She must first mar
Her flaming wear,
And after fall, for in her dress
Of glory, she cannot transgress.

Man of old
Within the line
Of Eden could
Like the Sun shine
All naked, innocent and bright,
And intimate with Heav'n, as light;

But since he
That brightness soil'd,
His garments be
All dark and spoil'd,
And here are left as nothing worth,
Till the Refiners fire breaks forth.

Then comes he!

Whose mighty light
Made his cloathes be
Like Heav'n, all bright;
The Fuller, whose pure blood did flow
To make stain'd man more white then snow.

Hee alone
And none else can
Bring bone to bone
And rebuild man,
And by his all subduing might
Make clay ascend more quick then light.

¶

They are all gone into the world of light!
    And I alone sit lingring here;
Their very memory is fair and bright,
    And my sad thoughts doth clear.

It glows and glitters in my cloudy brest
    Like stars upon some gloomy grove,
Or those faint beams in which this hill is drest,
    After the Sun's remove.

I see them walking in an Air of glory,
    Whose light doth trample on my days:
My days, which are at best but dull and hoary,
    Meer glimering and decays.

O holy hope! and high humility,
    High as the Heavens above!
These are your walks, and you have shew'd them me
    To kindle my cold love,

Dear, beauteous death! the Jewel of the Just,
    Shining nowhere, but in the dark;
What mysteries do lie beyond thy dust;

Could man outlook that mark!

He that hath found some fledg'd birds nest, may know
    At first sight, if the bird be flown;
But what fair Well, or Grove he sings in now,
    That is to him unknown.

And yet, as Angels in some brighter dreams
    Call to the soul, when man doth sleep:
So some strange thoughts transcend our wonted theams,
    And into glory peep.

If a star were confin'd into a Tomb
    Her captive flames must needs burn there;
But when the hand that lockt her up, gives room,
    She'l shine through all the sphaere.

O Father of eternal life, and all
    Created glories under thee!
Resume thy spirit from this world of thrall
    Into true liberty.

Either disperse these mists, which blot and fill
    My perspective (still) as they pass,
Or else remove me hence unto that hill,
    Where I shall need no glass.

Cock-crowing

Father of lights! what Sunnie seed,
What glance of day hast thou confin'd
Into this bird? To all the breed
This busie Ray thou hast assign'd;
      Their magnetisme works all night,
      And dreams of Paradise and light.

Their eyes watch for the morning hue,
Their little grain expelling night
So shines and sings, as if it knew
The path unto the house of light.
        It seems their candle, howe'r done,
        Was tinn'd and lighted at the sunne.

If such a tincture, such a touch,
So firm a longing can impowre
Shall thy own image think it much
To watch for thy appearing hour?
        If a meer blast so fill the sail,
        Shall not the breath of God prevail?

O thou immortall light and heat!
Whose hand so shines through all this frame,
That by the beauty of the seat,
We plainly see, who made the same.
        Seeing thy seed abides in me,
        Dwell thou in it, and I in thee.

To sleep without thee, is to die;
Yea, 'tis a death partakes of hell:
For where thou dost not close the eye
It never opens, I can tell.
        In such a dark, AEgyptian border,
        The shades of death dwell and disorder.

If joyes, and hopes, and earnest throws,
And hearts, whose Pulse beats still for light
Are given to birds; who, but thee, knows
A love-sick souls exalted flight?
        Can souls be track'd by any eye
        But his, who gave them wings to flie?

Onely this Veyle which thou hast broke,
And must be broken yet in me,
This veyle, I say, is all the cloke

And cloud which shadows thee from me.
        This veyle thy full-ey'd love denies,
        And onely gleams and fractions spies.

O take it off! make no delay,
But brush me with thy light, that I
May shine unto a perfect day,
And warme me at thy glorious Eye!
        O take it off! or till it flee,
        Though with no Lilie, stay with me!

The Starre

What ever 'tis, whose beauty here below
Attracts thee thus & makes thee stream & flow,
        And wind and curle, and wink and smile,
        Shifting thy gate and guile:

Though thy close commerce nought at all imbarrs
My present search, for Eagles eye not starrs,
        And still the lesser by the best
        And highest good is blest:

Yet, seeing all things that subsist and be,
Have their Commissions from Divinitie,
        And teach us duty, I will see
        What man may learn from thee.

First, I am sure, the Subject so respected
Is well disposed, for bodies once infected,
        Deprav'd or dead, can have with thee
        No hold, nor sympathie.

Next, there's in it a restless, pure desire
And longing for thy bright and vitall fire,
        Desire that never will be quench'd,
        Nor can be writh'd, nor wrench'd.

These are the Magnets which so strongly move
And work all night upon thy light and love,
    As beauteous shapes, we know not why,
      Command and guide the eye.

For where desire, celestiall, pure desire
Hath taken root, and grows, and doth not tire,
    There God a Commerce states, and sheds
      His Secret on their heads.

This is the Heart he craves; and who so will
But give it him, and grudge not; he shall feel
    That God is true, as herbs unseen
      Put on their youth and green.

The Bird

Hither thou com'st: the busie wind all night
Blew through thy lodging, where thy own warm wing
Thy pillow was. Many a sullen storm
(For which course man seems much the fitter born,)
    Rain'd on thy bed
    And harmless head.

And now as fresh and chearful as the light
Thy little heart in early hymns doth sing
Unto that *Providence,* whose unseen arm
Curb'd them, and cloath'd thee well and warm.
    All things that be, praise him; and had
    Their lesson taught them, when first made.

So hills and valleys into singing break,
And though poor stones have neither speech nor tongue,
While active winds and streams both run and speak,
Yet stones are deep in admiration.
Thus Praise and Prayer here beneath the Sun
Make lesser mornings, when the great are done.

62

For each inclosed Spirit is a star
    Inlightning his own little sphaere,
Whose light, though fetcht and borrowed from far,
    Both mornings makes, and evenings there.

But as these Birds of light make a land glad,
Chirping their solemn Matins on each tree:
So in the shades of night some dark fowls be,
Whose heavy notes make all that hear them, sad.

    The Turtle then in Palm-trees mourns,
        While Owls and Satyrs howl;
    The pleasant Land to brimstone turns
        And all her streams grow foul.

Brightness and mirth, and love and faith, all flye,
Till the Day-spring breaks forth again from high.

The Knot

    Bright Queen of Heaven! Gods Virgin Spouse
        The glad worlds blessed maid!
    Whose beauty tyed life to thy house,
        And brought us saving ayd.

    Thou art the true Loves-knot; by thee
        God is made our Allie,
    And mans inferior Essence he
        With his did dignifie.

    For Coalescent by that Band
        We are his body grown,
    Nourished with favors from his hand
        Whom for our head we own.

    And such a Knot, what arm dares loose,
        What life, what death can sever?

Which us in him, and him in us
United keeps for ever.

The Seed growing secretly
S. Mark 4. 26

If this worlds friends might see but once
What some poor man may often feel,
Glory, and gold, and Crowns and Thrones
They would soon quit and learn to kneel.

My dew, my dew! my early love,
My souls bright food, thy absence kills!
Hover not long, eternal Dove!
Life without thee is loose and spills.

Somthing I had, which long ago
Did learn to suck, and sip, and taste,
But now grown sickly, sad and slow,
Doth fret and wrangle, pine and waste.

O spred thy sacred wings and shake
One living drop! one drop life keeps!
If pious griefs Heavens joys awake,
O fill his bottle! thy childe weeps!

Slowly and sadly doth he grow,
And soon as left, shrinks back to ill;
O feed that life, which makes him blow
And spred and open to thy will!

For thy eternal, living wells
None stain'd or wither'd shall come near:
A fresh, immortal green there dwells,
And spotless *white* is all the wear.

Dear, secret *Greenness*! nurst below

64

Tempests and windes, and winter nights,
Vex not, that but one sees thee grow,
That *One* made all these lesser lights.

If those bright joys he singly sheds
On thee, were all met in one Crown,
Both Sun and Stars would hide their heads;
And Moons, though full, would get them down.

Let glory be their bait, whose mindes
Are all too high for a low Cell:
Though Hawks can prey through storms and winds,
The poor Bee in her hive must dwel.

Glory, the Crouds cheap tinsel still
To what most takes them, is a drudge;
And they too oft take good for ill,
And thriving vice for vertue judge.

What needs a Conscience calm and bright
Within it self an outward test?
Who breaks his glass to take more light,
Makes way for storms into his rest.

Then bless thy secret growth, nor catch
At noise, but thrive unseen and dumb;
Keep clean, bear fruit, earn life and watch
Till the white winged Reapers come!

¶

As time one day by me did pass
    Through a large dusky glasse
    He held, I chanc'd to look
    And spyed his curious book
Of past days, where sad Heav'n did shed
A mourning light upon the dead.

E

Many disordered lives I saw
    And foul records which thaw
    My kinde eyes still, but in
    A fair, white page of thin
And ev'n, smooth lines, like the Suns rays,
Thy name was writ, and all thy days.

O bright and happy Kalendar!
    Where youth shines like a star
    All pearl'd with tears, and may
    Teach age, *The Holy way;*
Where through thick pangs, high agonies
Faith into life breaks, and death dies.

As some meek *night-piece* which day quails,
    To candle-light unveils:
    So by one beamy line
    From thy bright lamp did shine,
In the same page thy humble grave
Set with green herbs, glad hopes and brave.

Here slept my thoughts dear mark! which dust
    Seem'd to devour, like rust;
    But dust (I did observe)
    By hiding doth preserve,
As we for long and sure recruits,
Candy with sugar our choice fruits.

O calm and sacred bed where lies
    In deaths dark mysteries
    A beauty far more bright
    Then the noons cloudless light
For whose dry dust green branches bud
And robes are bleach'd in the *Lambs* blood.

Sleep happy ashes! (blessed sleep!)
    While haplesse I still weep;
    Weep that I have out-liv'd

66

My life, and unreliev'd
Must (soul-lesse shadow!) so live on,
Though life be dead, and my joys gone.

Childe-hood

I cannot reach it; and my striving eye
Dazles at it, as at eternity.
　　Were now that Chronicle alive,
Those white designs which children drive,
And the thoughts of each harmless hour,
With their content too in my pow'r,
Quickly would I make my path even,
And by meer playing go to Heaven.

　　　　Why should men love
A Wolf, more then a Lamb or Dove?
Or choose hell-fire and brimstone streams
Before bright stars, and Gods own beams?
Who kisseth thorns, will hurt his face,
But flowers do both refresh and grace,
And sweetly living (*fie on men!*)
Are when dead, medicinal then.
If seeing much should make staid eyes,
And long experience should make wise;
Since all that age doth teach, is ill,
Why should I not love childe-hood still?
Why if I see a rock or shelf,
Shall I from thence cast down my self,
Or by complying with the world,
From the same precipice be hurl'd?
Those observations are but foul
Which make me wise to lose my soul.

And yet the *Practice* worldlings call
Business and weighty action all,
Checking the poor childe for his play,

But gravely cast themselves away.

Dear, harmless age! the short, swift span,
Where weeping virtue parts with man;
Where love without lust dwells, and bends
What way we please, without self-ends.

An age of mysteries! which he
Must live twice, that would Gods face see;
Which *Angels* guard, and with it play,
Angels! which foul men drive away.

How do I study now, and scan
Thee, more then ere I studyed man,
And onely see through a long night
Thy edges, and thy bordering light!
O for thy Center and mid-day!
For sure that is the *narrow way*.

The Night
John 2.3

Through that pure *Virgin-shrine*,
That sacred vail drawn o'r thy glorious noon
That men might look and live as Glo-worms shine,
And face the Moon:
Wise *Nicodemus* saw such light
As made him know his God by night,

Most blest believer he!
Who in that land of darkness and blinde eyes
Thy long expected healing wings could see,
When thou didst rise,
And what can never more be done,
Did at mid-night speak with the Sun!

O who will tell me, where

He found thee at that dead and silent hour!
What hallow'd solitary ground did bear
        So rare a flower,
        Within whose sacred leafs did lie
        The fulnes of the Deity.

        No mercy-seat of gold,
No dead and dusty *Cherub*, nor carv'd stone,
But his own living works did my Lord hold
        And lodge alone;
        Where *trees* and *herbs* did watch and peep
        And wonder, while the *Jews* did sleep.

        Dear night! this worlds defeat;
The stop to busie fools; cares check and curb;
The day of Spirits; my souls calm retreat
        Which none disturb!
        Christs *progress, and his prayer time;
        The hours to which high Heaven doth chime.

        Gods silent, searching flight:
When my Lords head is fill'd with dew, and all
His locks are wet with the clear drops of night;
        His still, soft call;
        His knocking time; The souls dumb watch,
        When Spirits their fair kinred catch.

        Were all my loud, evil days
Calm and unhaunted as is thy dark Tent,
Whose peace but by some *Angels* wing or voice
        Is seldom rent;
        Then I in Heaven all the long year
        Would keep, and never wander here.

        But living where the Sun
Doth all things wake, and when all mix and tyre
Themselves and others, I consent and run
        To ev'ry myre,

And by this worlds ill-guiding light,
Erre more then I can do by night.

There is in God (some say)
A deep, but dazling darkness; As men here
Say it is late and dusky, because they
See not all clear;
O for that night! where I in him
Might live invisible and dim.

*Mark, chap. 1.35. S. Luke, chap. 21. 37.

Death

Though since thy first sad entrance by
Just *Abels* blood,
'Tis now six thousand years well nigh,
And still thy sov'rainty holds good:
Yet by none art thou understood.

We talk and name thee with much ease
As a tryed thing,
And every one can slight his lease
As if it ended in a Spring,
Which shades & bowers doth rent-free bring.

To thy dark land these heedless go:
But there was *One*,
Who search'd it quite through to and fro,
And then returning, like the Sun,
Discover'd all, that there is done.

And since his death, we throughly see
All thy dark way;
Thy shades but thin and narrow be,
Which his first looks will quickly fray:
Mists make but triumphs for the day.

70

As harmless violets, which give
                Their virtues here
For salves and syrups, while they live,
Do after calmly disappear,
And neither grieve, repine, nor fear:

So dye his servants; and as sure
                Shall they revive.
Then let not dust your eyes obscure,
But lift them up, where still alive,
Though fled from you, their spirits hive.

The Water-fall

With what deep murmurs through times silent stealth
Doth thy transparent, cool and watry wealth
           Here flowing fall,
           And chide, and call,
As if his liquid, loose Retinue staid
Lingring, and were of this steep place afraid,
           The common pass
           Where, clear as glass,
           All must descend
           Not to an end:
But quickned by this deep and rocky grave,
Rise to a longer course more bright and brave.
Dear stream! dear bank, where often I
Have sate, and pleas'd my pensive eye,
Why, since each drop of thy quick store
Runs thither, whence it flow'd before,
Should poor souls fear a shade or night,
Who came (sure) from a sea of light?
Or since those drops are all sent back
So sure to thee, that none doth lack,
Why should frail flesh doubt any more

71

That what God takes, hee'l not restore?
O useful Element and clear!
My sacred wash and cleanser here,
My first consigner unto those
Fountains of life, where the Lamb goes?
What sublime truths, and wholesome themes,
Lodge in thy mystical, deep streams!
Such as dull man can never finde
Unless that Spirit lead his minde,
Which first upon thy face did move,
And hatch'd all with his quickning love.
As this loud brooks incessant fall
In streaming rings restagnates all,
Which reach by course the bank, and then
Are no more seen, just so pass men.
O my invisible estate,
My glorious liberty, still late!
Thou art the Channel my soul seeks,
Not this with Cataracts and Creeks.

Quickness

False life! a foil and no more, when
          Wilt thou be gone?
Thou foul deception of all men
That would not have the true come on.

Thou art a Moon-like toil; a blinde
          Self-posing state;
A dark contest of waves and winde;
A meer tempestuous debate.

Life is a fix'd, discerning light,
          A knowing Joy;
No chance, or fit: but ever bright,
And calm and full, yet doth not cloy.

'Tis such a blissful thing, that still
                    Doth vivifie,
And shine and smile, and hath the skill
To please without Eternity.

Thou art a toylsom Mole, or less
                    A moving mist
But life is, what none can express,
A quickness, which my God hath kist.

The Queer

O tell me whence that joy doth spring
Whose diet is divine and fair,
Which wears heaven, like a bridal ring,
And tramples on doubts and despair?

Whose Eastern traffique deals in bright
And boundless Empyrean themes,
Mountains of spice, Day-stars and light,
Green trees of life, and living streams?

Tell me, O tell who did thee bring
And here, without my knowledge, plac'd,
Till thou didst grow and get a wing,
A wing with eyes, and eyes that taste?

Sure, *holyness* the *Magnet* is,
And *Love* the *Lure*, that woos thee down;
Which makes the high transcendent bliss
Of knowing thee, so rarely known.

The Book

Eternal God! maker of all
That have liv'd here, since the mans fall;

The Rock of ages! in whose shade
They live unseen, when here they fade.

Thou knew'st this *papyr*, when it was
Meer *seed*, and after that but *grass*;
Before 'twas *drest* or *spun*, and when
Made *linen*, who did *wear* it then:
What were their lifes, their thoughts & deeds
Whither good *corn*, or fruitless *weeds*.

Thou knew'st this *Tree*, when a green *shade*
Cover'd it, since a *Cover* made,
And where it flourish'd, grew and spread,
As if it never should be dead.

Thou knew'st this harmless *beast*, when he
Did live and feed by thy decree
On each green thing; then slept (well fed)
Cloath'd with this *skin*, which now lies spred
A *Covering* o're this aged book,
Which makes me wisely weep and look
On my own dust; meer dust it is,
But not so·dry and clean as this.
Thou knew'st and saw'st them all and though
Now scatter'd thus, dost know them so.

O knowing, glorious spirit! when
Thou shalt restore trees, beasts and men,
When thou shalt make all new again,
Destroying onely death and pain,
Give him amongst thy works a place,
Who in them lov'd and sought thy face!

Notes

'To my worthy friend Master T. Lewes'

Title: Thomas Lewes was Rector of Llanfigan, across the river Usk from Vaughan's home in Newton.
bottome: a skein or ball of thread.

'Boethius, *De Consolatione Philosophiae, Lib II,Metrum 5*'

This is one of thirteen translations from Boethius included in *Olor Iscanus.* Cf. Vaughan's own poems 'The Retreate' and 'Childe-hood'.

Mast: acorns, a staple of the Golden Age.

'Vanity of Spirit'

drills: rivulets or small streams.

'Come, come, what doe I here?'

This poem, like several untitled ones which follow, appears to be an elegy for the poet's younger brother William. See Introduction.

'Midnight'

Ejections: in the obsolete sense of outgoings of emotion.

'Content'

curl'd, puff'd points: lace arranged elaborately to adorn a costume.
story: head-dress (?).

'The Storm'

use: moral; practical application.

'Silence, and stealth of dayes!'

one Pearle: traditionally glossed as the bible.

'The Passion'

two small mites: Cf. the poor widow's offering, Mark 12:42.

'And do they so?'

Rom. Cap. 8, ver. 19: In the A. V., 'For the earnest expectation of the creature waiteth for the manifestation of the sons of God.' But Vaughan heads his poem with the more vivid rendering of Beza's Latin New Testament, which adds the phrase 'exerto Capite': 'For created things *with lifted head* watch for the appearing of the sons of God.'
Influence: the control which Heaven exerts over even inanimate beings.
newes: trifling novelties; or, idle conversation.

'Corruption'

Angels lay Leiger: i.e. they dwelled as resident ambassadors.
Thrust in thy sickle: The cry in Rev. 14:18 announcing the harvest of the wrath of God in the Day of Judgement.

'The Tempest'

Issacher: In Jacob's prophecy (Gen. 49), Issacher is the father of a nation of servants, 'a strong ass couching down between two burdens'.

'The Constellation'

Clue: ball of thread which may lead a man out of a maze. The word is used with similar force in 'Son-days'.
slips his span: wastes his life in idleness.
that Lamb which had the Dragons voice: the beast in Rev. 13 who 'deceiveth them that dwell on the earth'. The reference to the Puritans is fairly transparent.

'Man'

some stones: Probably lodestones, but Vaughan may again be ascribing sentience to inanimate objects, as in 'And do they so?'

'Ascension-Hymn'

The Fuller: Cf. the Messianic prophecy in Malachi, especially 3:2: 'But who may abide the day of his coming? and who shall stand when he appeareth? for he is like a refiner's fire, and like fuller's sope.'

'They are all gone into the world of light!'

perspective: telescope.

'Cock-crowing'

tinn'd: kindled.
Though with no Lilie: Cf. Matt. 6:28 ff: 'Consider the lilies of the
field . . . if God so clothe the grass of the field, which to day is, and
to morrow is cast into the oven, shall he not much more clothe you,
O ye of little faith?'

'The Starre'

commerce; As in 'Cock-crowing', Vaughan exploits the Hermetic
idea that earthly creatures are influenced in their nature,
development and behaviour by their counterparts in the celestial
sphere.

'The Knot'

true Loves-knot: a knot of two loops symbolizing fidelity in love.

'The Seed growing secretly'

S. Mark 4.26: 'So is the kingdom of God, as if a man should cast
seed into the ground.'
Reapers: In Matt. 13 the same parable is given a point-by-point
interpretation (vv. 37-43). See especially v. 39: '. . . the harvest is
the end of this world; and the reapers are the angels.'

'As time one day by me did pass'

night-piece: A puzzle: Vaughan speaks of a picture which shows to
better advantage by candlelight than by daylight. But I can find no
precedent for this use of 'night-piece', which normally means
simply a painting of a night scene.

'Childe-hood'

Practice: scheme, plot, intrigue.

'The Night'

John 2.3: A mistake; Vaughan intends John 3:2. The story of the colloquy with Nicodemus, who 'came to Jesus by night', fills the first twenty-one verses of the third chapter of the Gospel.

'The Water-fall'

Retinue: accented on the second syllable in Vaughan's day.
restagnates: becomes or remains stagnant.

'The Queer'

Title: meaning 'query'.
A wing with eyes: Cf. the four beasts symbolizing the Evangelists in Rev. 4:8: 'And the four beasts had each of them six wings about him; and they were full of eyes within: and they rest not day and night, saying, Holy, holy, holy, Lord God Almighty, which was, and is, and is to come.'
eyes that taste: Cf. Psalm 34:8: 'O taste and see that the Lord is good.'

Acknowledgements

The text of this selection is based on *The Works of Henry Vaughan* (2nd ed.), ed. L. C. Martin (Oxford, 1957). Martin's notes are thorough and authoritative. A more recent annotated edition, excluding prose, is provided by *The Complete Poetry of Henry Vaughan,* ed. French Fogle (New York, 1964). The standard biography is *Henry Vaughan: A Life and Interpretation,* by F. E. Hutchinson (Oxford, 1947). I could net have written my introduction without the aid of this book, which also contains valuable critical passages. Some other relevant titles should be noted:

R. A. Durr, *On the Mystical Poetry of Henry Vaughan,* Cambridge, Mass., 1962.

Ross Garner, *Henry Vaughan: Experience and the Tradition,* Chicago, 1959.

Elizabeth Holmes, *Henry Vaughan and the Hermetic Philosophy,* Oxford, 1932.

E. C. Pettit, *Of Paradise and Light: A Study of Vaughan's* Silex Scintillans, Cambridge, 1960.

James D. Simmonds, *Masques of God: Form and Theme in the Poetry of Henry Vaughan,* Pittsburgh, 1972.

Especially useful shorter interpretations appear in *Poetry and Humanism,* by M. M. Mahood (London, 1950) and *The Paradise Within,* by Louis L. Martz (New Haven, 1964).

Following the practice of this series, I have kept my annotation to modest proportions. I have glossed obsolete or exceptionally uncommon words and identified some of Vaughan's allusions, which are chiefly biblical. Since it is not possible to note every biblical echo in a book of this size, I have commented only on those references which are crucial to the meaning of a poem or which stand out from their context in so riddling a way as to impede the reader's progress.

It is a pleasure to acknowledge the aid of colleagues and friends by which this book has profited. Professor Michael Holahan read a draft of the introduction and offered many improving suggestions. Jonathan and Valerie Kamholtz provided a note to one of the poems, as did the Rev. David W. Boulton in another case. To Fr Boulton I am more generally indebted for much good counsel during the time in which this volume was being readied for the press.